26 letters and 99 cents

BY TANA HOBAN

GREENWILLOW BOOKS
An Imprint of HarperCollinsPublishers

This one is for Candace

Soft Touch letters and numbers used in this book are available
at most toy stores or through International Playthings Inc.,
116 Washington Street, Bloomfield, NJ 07003.

The photographs were reproduced from 35-mm slides
and printed in full-color.

Manufactured in China.
First Edition   13 14 SCP 20 19 18 17 16

Library of Congress Cataloging-in-Publication Data

Hoban, Tana. 26 letters and 99 cents.
"Greenwillow Books."
Summary: Color photographs of letters, numbers,
coins, and common objects introduce the alphabet,
coinage, and the counting system.
1. English language—Alphabet—Juvenile literature.
2. Counting—Juvenile literature. [1. Alphabet.
2. Counting. 3. Coins] I. Title.
II. Title: Twenty-six letters and ninety-nine cents.
PE1155.H57 1987 [E] 86-11993
ISBN 0-688-06361-6 (trade). ISBN 0-688-06362-4 (lib. bdg.)
ISBN 0-688-14389-X (paperback).

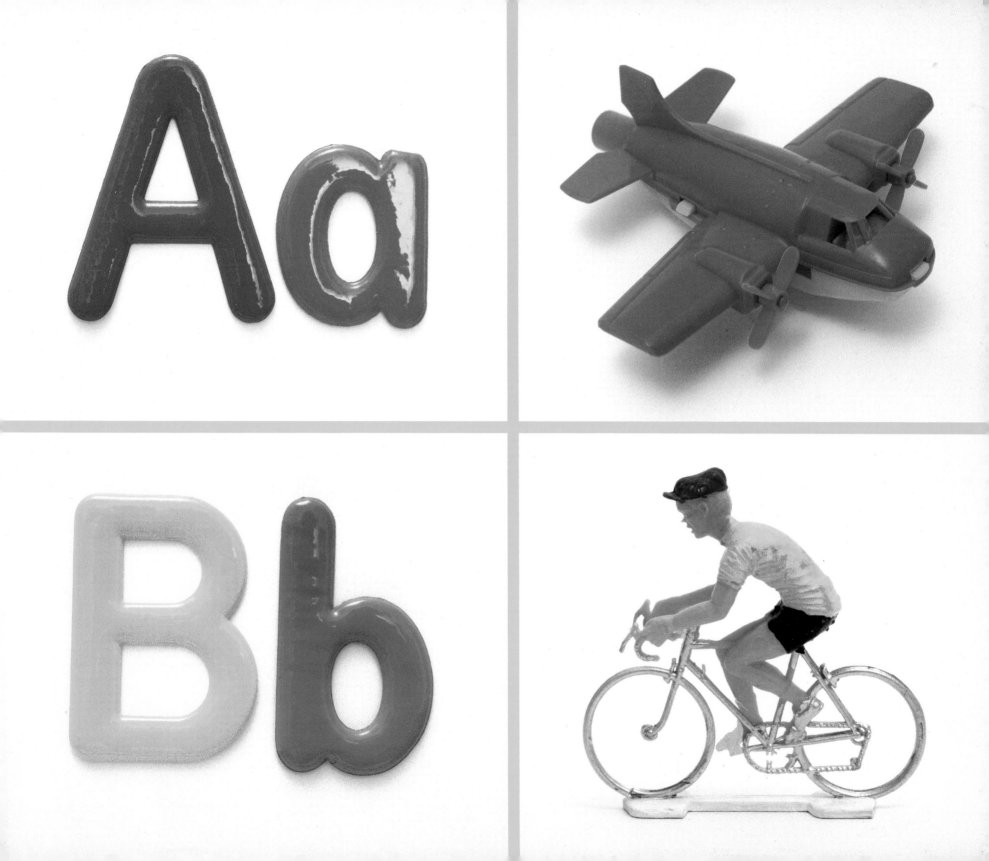

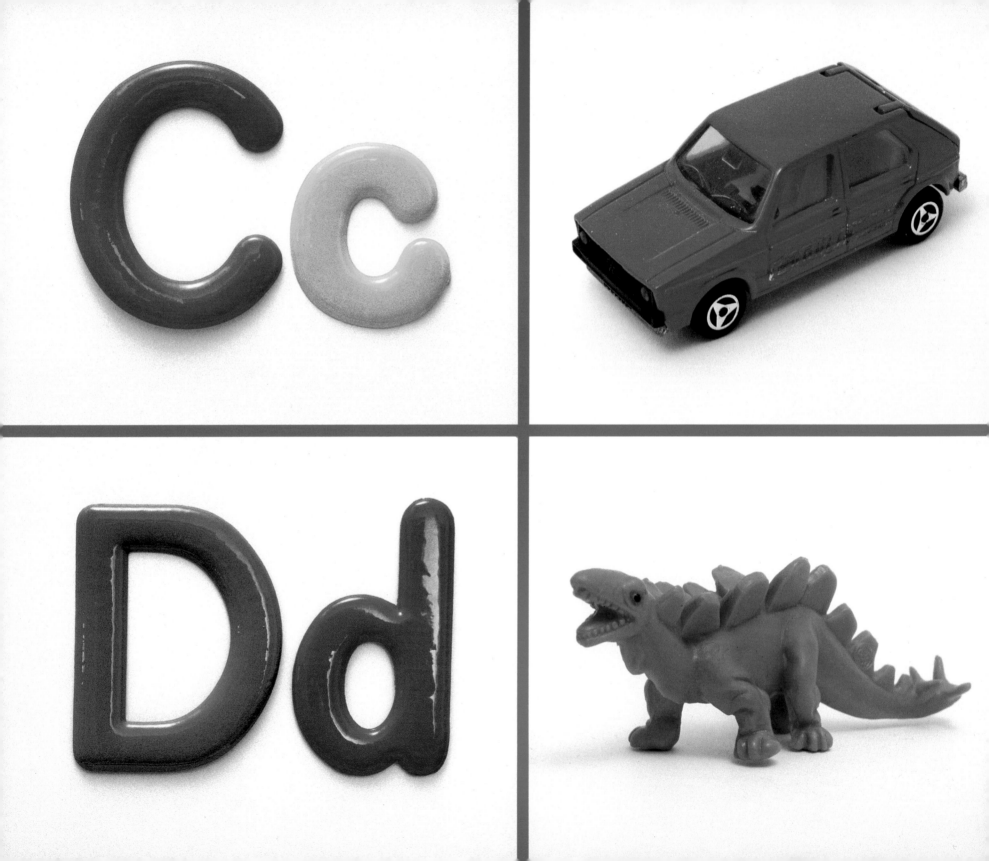

C c

D d

Uu

Vv

BE MY VALENTINE

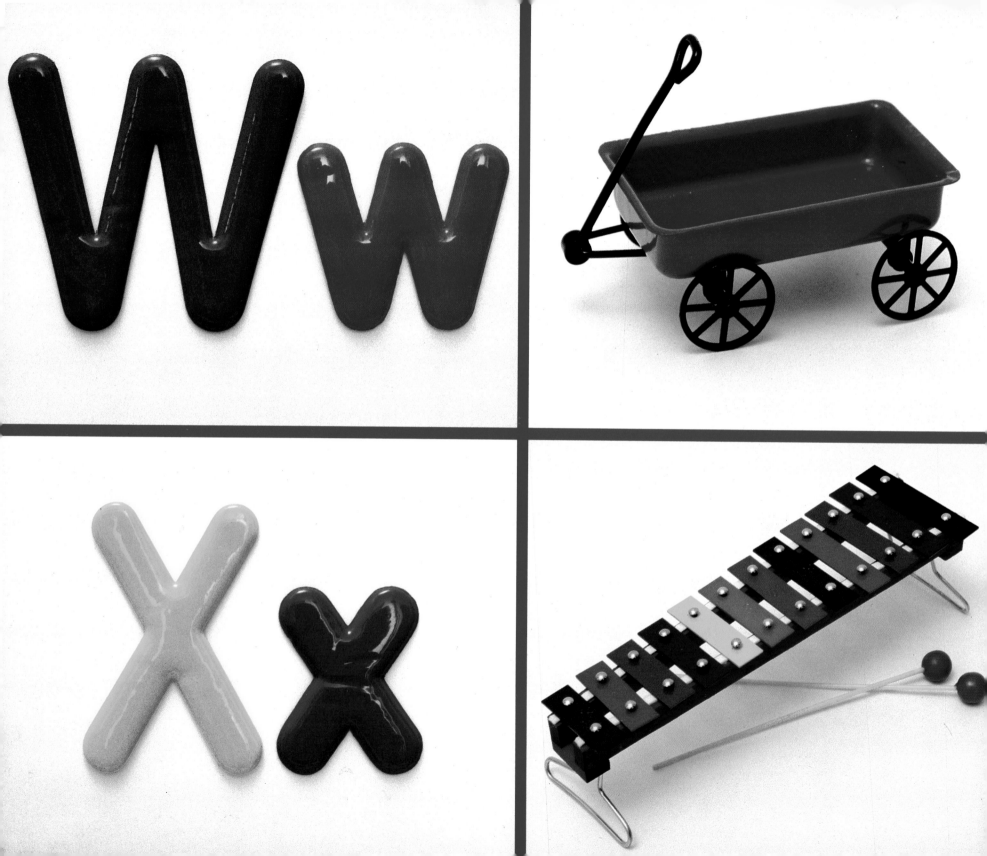

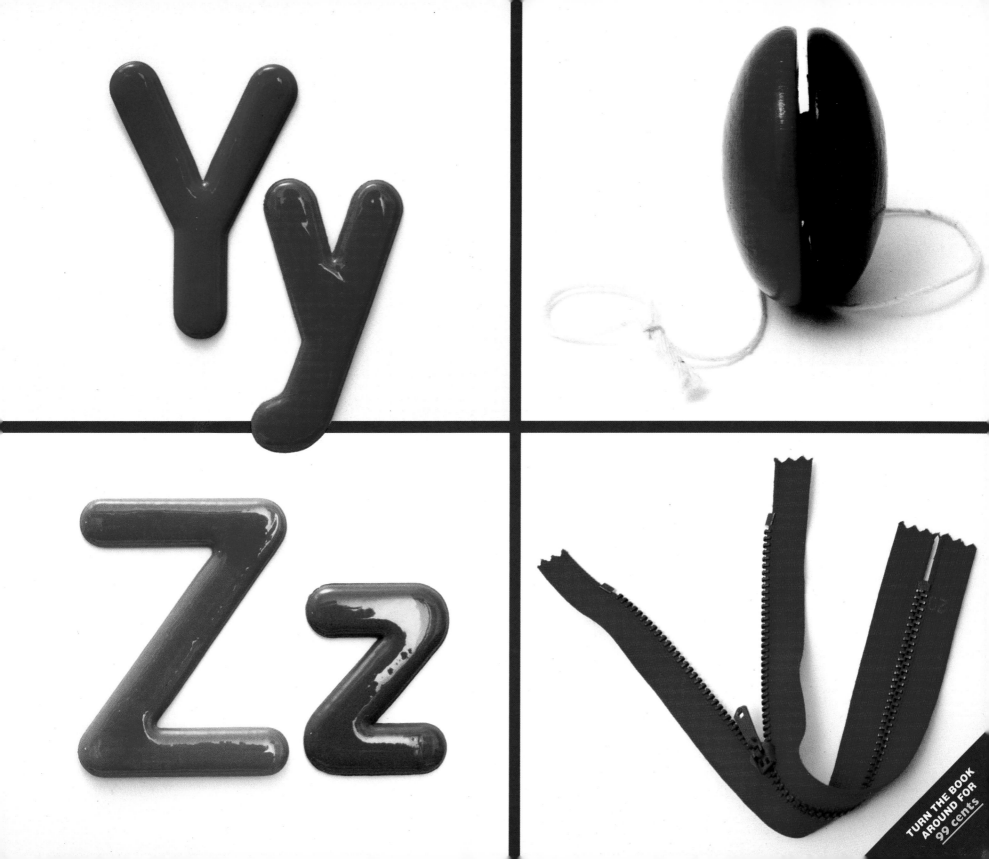

Yy

Zz

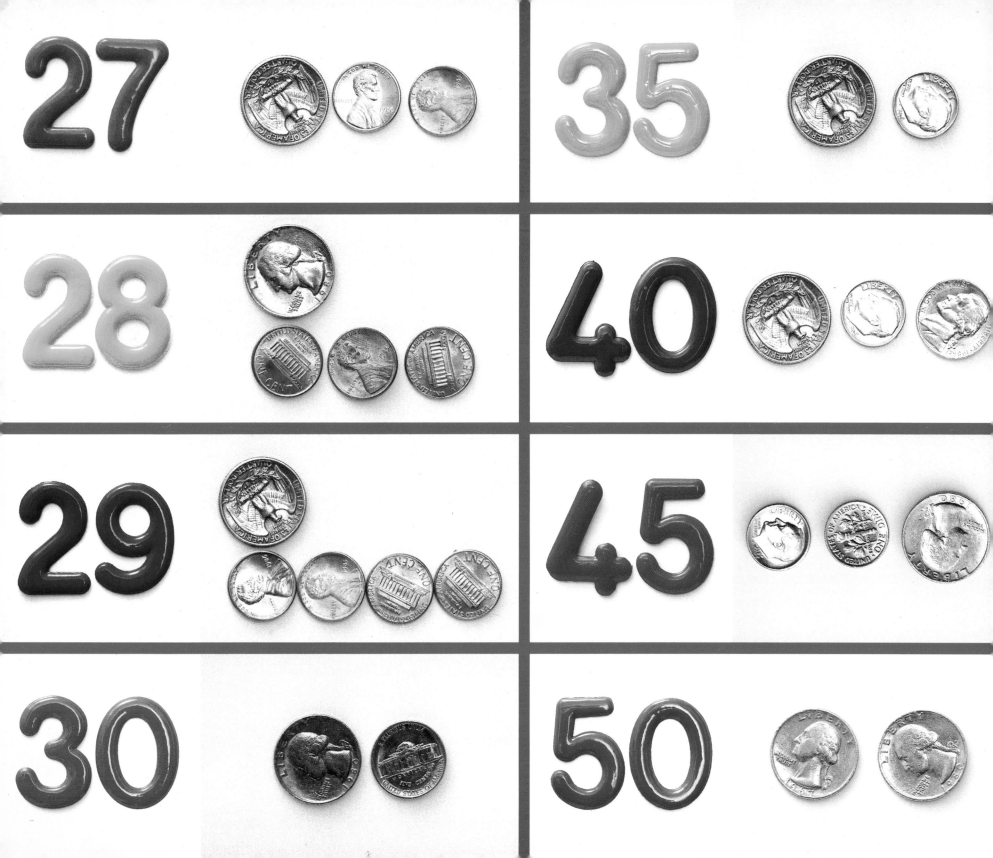

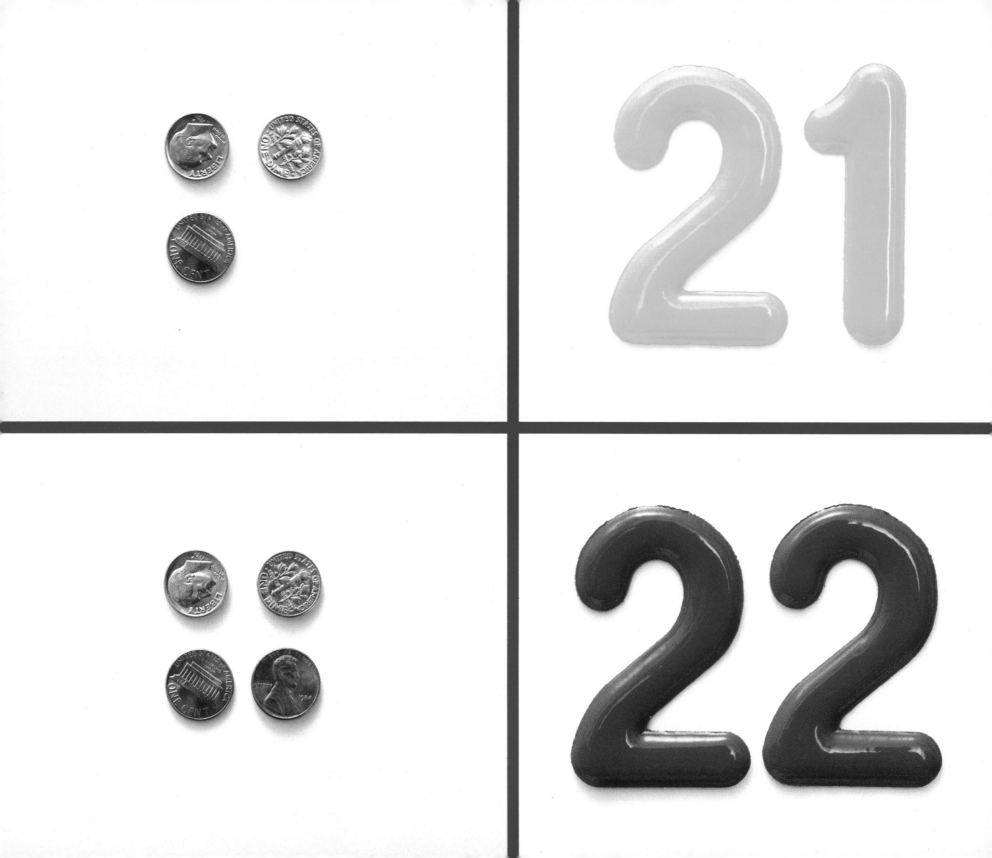

21

22

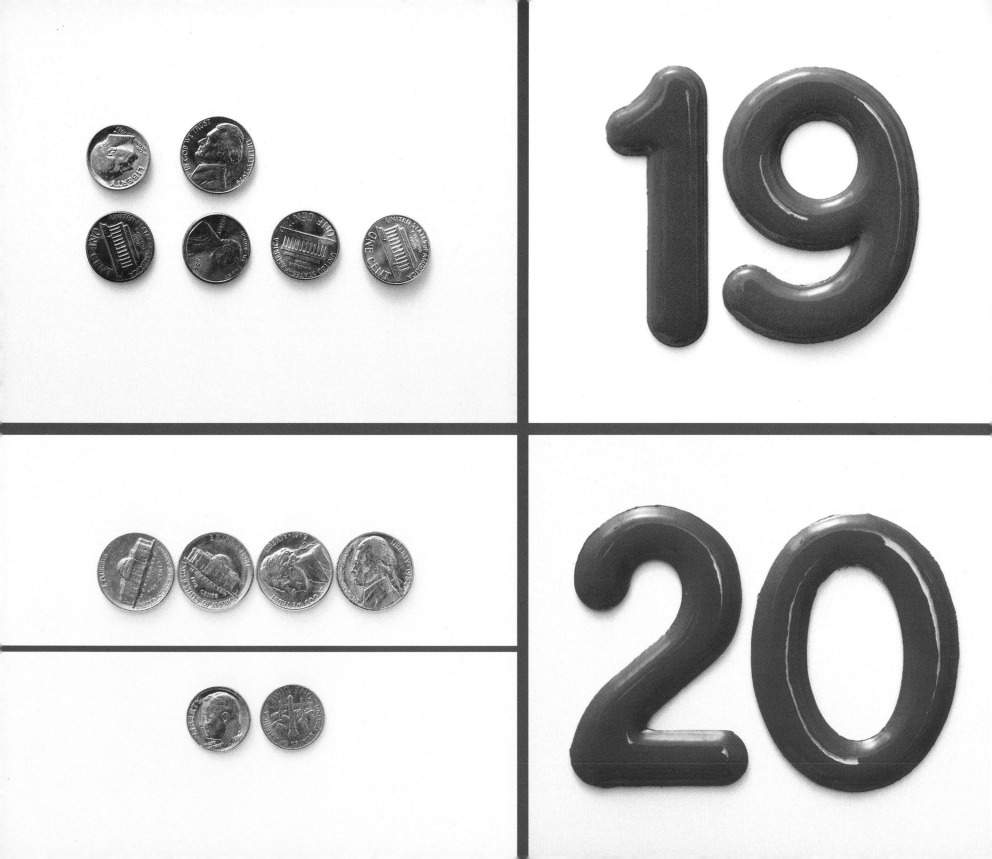

15

16

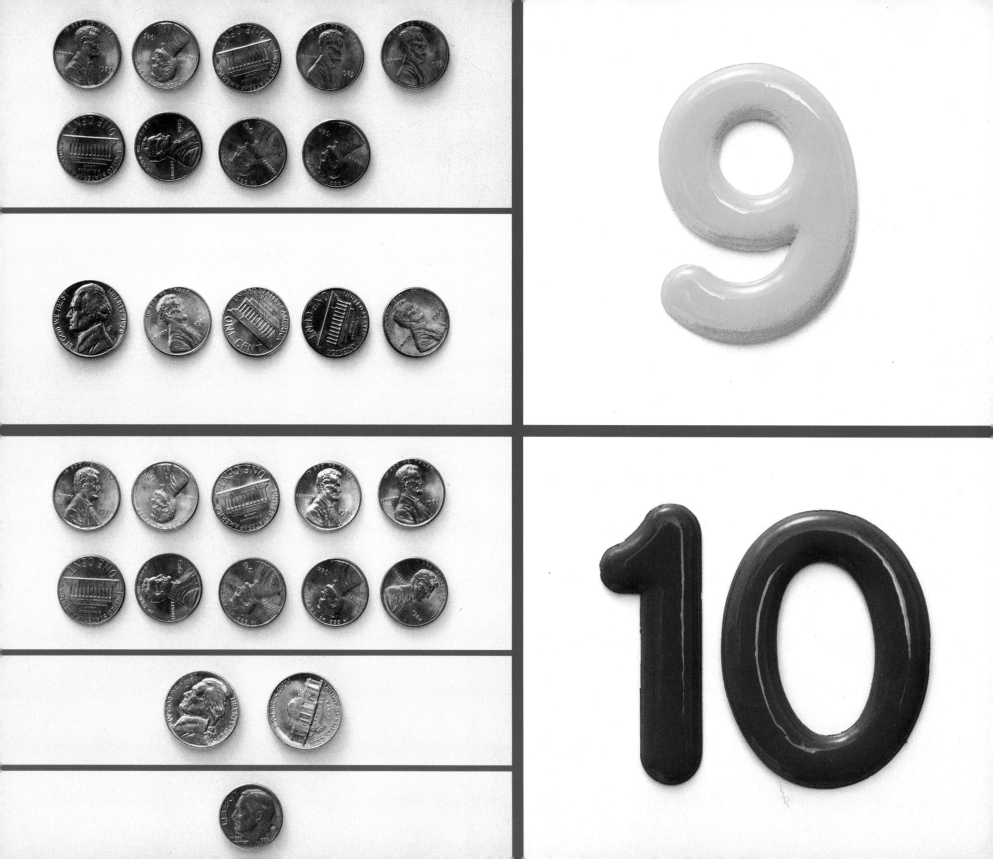

This one is for Candace

Soft Touch letters and numbers used in this book are available
at most toy stores or through International Playthings Inc.,
116 Washington Street, Bloomfield, NJ 07003.

The photographs were reproduced from 35-mm slides
and printed in full-color.

Manufactured in China.
First Edition   13 14 SCP 20 19 18 17 16

Library of Congress Cataloging-in-Publication Data

Hoban, Tana. 26 letters and 99 cents.
"Greenwillow Books."
Summary: Color photographs of letters, numbers,
coins, and common objects introduce the alphabet,
coinage, and the counting system.
1. English language—Alphabet—Juvenile literature.
2. Counting—Juvenile literature. [1. Alphabet.
2. Counting. 3. Coins] I. Title.
II. Title: Twenty-six letters and ninety-nine cents.
PE1155.H57 1987 [E] 86-11993
ISBN 0-688-06361-6 (trade). ISBN 0-688-06362-4 (lib. bdg.)
ISBN 0-688-14389-X (paperback).

26 letters and 99 cents

BY TANA HOBAN

GREENWILLOW BOOKS
An Imprint of HarperCollinsPublishers